PORTFOLIO 5

METROPOLITAN SEMINARS IN ART

Portfolio 5 · *Composition*

by John Canaday

CHIEF OF THE DIVISION OF EDUCATION

THE PHILADELPHIA MUSEUM OF ART

THE METROPOLITAN MUSEUM OF ART

COMPOSITION
Pictures as Patterns

IN OUR discussions of realism, expressionism, and abstraction we have been dealing with the painter's point of view toward his subject matter. First we saw the realist reflecting the world in its own terms, but in many different ways, since those terms themselves differ according to the time and the place we live in. We saw that the expressionist, in contrast, is less interested in reflecting the world around us than in revealing his emotional reactions to it. He explores these emotions in a personal and subjective way. Finally, the abstractionist is interested neither in reproducing the look of things, like the realist, nor primarily in exhibiting his emotional reactions to them, like the expressionist. He is first of all interested in considering the world as a complex of ideas.

Thus the realist, painting a tree, would give us a fairly accurate reproduction of the way the tree looks, leaving to us the emotional or intellectual reaction. The expressionist, taking the same tree, would distort its form and color as he pleased in order to tell us how he felt about it. The abstractionist, after asking himself what the main idea of a tree might be, would proceed to intellectualize the forms of nature into a pattern revealing that idea.

Of course, these three approaches are bound to overlap. We saw that there is hardly such a thing as a purely realistic painting or a purely expressionist or a purely abstract one. The eye, the emotions, and the intellect all must share in the creation of every painting—and in

its enjoyment, too. Even the most visually pleasing or emotionally stimulating paintings have an abstract interest on a score that most observers miss—composition, the subject of this and our next two portfolios.

Composition is so important that we have already been dealing with it in most of the paintings discussed so far. When we analyzed the reasons for the curious disposition of the objects in Degas's *Woman with Chrysanthemums* (Plate 5, Portfolio 1), where the subject of the portrait was pushed far toward one edge of the canvas while the most conspicuous position was occupied by a large bouquet of flowers, we were showing how one of the most skillful pictorial composers of them all went about expressing his subject by compositional means. We referred frequently to "Whistler's Mother" as a combination of gray and black shapes arranged to create a mood. This is composition, or what might simply be called "arrangement."

Not every great painting is a great composition. But composition is so fundamental to the creation of pictures that a list of the world's greatest paintings would overlap a list of the greatest compositions in a majority of titles. Yet of all the elements in the art of painting, composition is the one least recognized by the average observer, even when it is playing a major part in his reaction to a picture.

It is perfectly possible to enjoy a painting without being aware of its composition. But our spontaneous enjoyment of subject, color, drawing, and emotional and intellectual expression are all deepened when we can recognize their interplay on a compositional basis.

In a general way compositions fall into two broad classifications, with every transitional stage between them. Two-dimensional compositions, which recognize the canvas for the flat surface it is, are limited to arrangements of lines and flat shapes on that surface. Three-dimensional compositions eliminate the canvas, so to speak, and open up the space behind it. We saw this distinction in the last portfolio in Picasso's *The Studio* (Plate 38) and a similar subject by Vermeer (Plate 37). We read the Picasso, which was quite flat, straight across the surface, but we looked into the depth of the Vermeer—into a cube of space created by the artist and occupied by the solid forms he arranged within it.

What enters into a painter's decision to conceive his painting in two dimensions or three? Ordinarily he may decide for himself, but occasionally the choice is dictated by special circumstances. If he is commissioned to do a mural painting, for instance, a painting actually covering the area of a wall as opposed to an independent picture merely hanging on the wall, his first obligation is to make his mural harmonize with the architecture.

Paintings and Walls

Americans visiting Europe for the first time are surprised to discover how many of the most familiar paintings are murals. A picture they have always known in a small reproduction, perhaps framed and hanging over a desk at home, turns out to be a vast affair covering the whole wall or ceiling it was painted on centuries ago. *The Journey of the Magi* by Benozzo Gozzoli, of which we reproduce an important section (Plate 49), well known and much beloved in miniature, is actually a mural painted from dado to ceiling around the walls of the family chapel in the Medici palace in Florence. The palace is a heavy stone structure, and the chapel interior shares in the feeling of solidity imparted by the thick walls.

Under certain circumstances it is all right for an artist to "eliminate" a wall by painting his mural in such a way that the space behind appears to open up. At other times, and more generally, a mural should lie flat on the wall, like a tapestry we might say, so that it does not affect the proportions of a room or leave us with the uncomfortable illusion that a heavy ceiling is left unsupported because the wall is painted out from under it. To avoid this illusion some muralists actually incorporate into their design painted supporting columns or arches through which we appear to look into the distance, but Gozzoli prefers to accept the wall for what it is, a solid supporting area. He treats *The Journey of the Magi* flatly and decoratively, as if it were ornamental wallpaper. He does not bother much with expressive factors; regarding himself first of all as a decorator, he is content to settle for ornamental richness. Some of the objects in his composition are nominally behind others, but we are not led into depth; we go up and down and across the wall, not into it. The mounted hunter pursuing a deer in the background is not painted as if he were far away. With a little imagination we can see horse and rider as a fluttering pennant attached to the spear in the foreground (see detail on cover). The rock shapes and tree shapes are designed for their interest as flat decorative shapes, not for their interest as representations of real rocks or trees and certainly not as solid forms receding into space. The multitude of forms and objects making up the picture are arranged tier upon tier up the wall (*Figure 1*), instead of layer behind layer into the distance. In short, the painting respects the integrity of the wall as an architectural element to the extent of playing second fiddle to the effectiveness of the room as a whole.

But many painters who are under no restrictions whatever still prefer to limit themselves

Figure 1

to two dimensions. Why is it that they do this?

The three-dimensional painter would argue that it is as foolish for a painter to limit himself to two dimensions as it is for a composer of music to limit himself to a few stringed instruments when he could write for a full symphony orchestra. But another painter might respond that Beethoven said as much in his quartets as he did in his symphonies, that Shakespeare said as much in the few lines of his sonnets as Balzac did in all the volumes of *La Comédie humaine*. And he would add that the economy of means, the compression of subject into a quartet or a sonnet or a two-dimensional painting, results in greater clarity and greater purity, and thus intensifies whatever the artist has to say. It was some such argument that Mondrian was making about

two-dimensional abstractions like *Rhythm of Straight Lines* (Plate 41, Portfolio 4). And the painter Maurice Denis, in a statement much quoted by other painters, once said, "Remember that a picture—before being a battle horse, a nude woman, or some anecdote —is essentially a plane surface covered with colors assembled in a certain order." The important words here are "plane surface." The implication is that there is a certain merit in recognizing its limitations and capitalizing on them.

Two-dimensional composition includes the most elementary as well as some of the most sophisticated approaches to painting. The least experienced of us, given a piece of paper, a pencil, and a model, would place our image in the center of the space rather than in one

7

corner. This is an instinctive recognition that a pictorial image needs a logical relationship to the flat area it occupies. We would also draw in two dimensions—necessarily, through ignorance of perspective and foreshortening and modeling, but also because the conception of space into the depth of a picture is a complicated one in itself. Yet even these elementary and unschooled approaches to the creation of a picture may produce a work of art when an artist's sensitivity is present, as in *Esther Tuttle* (Plate 50) by Joseph H. Davis, an untaught American painter of the last century.

A "Primitive" and a Sophisticate

In two-dimensional painting the artist's vocabulary is reduced to line, flat shape, and color. In each of these individual elements he must be inventive, but above all it is in their combination that he must be creative. Matisse, the great modern painter, once defined composition as "the art of arranging, in a decorative manner, the various elements at the artist's disposal." *Esther Tuttle* is a "primitive" painting—primitive in the new sense of the word meaning a painting by a self-taught, instinctively creative artist rather than an artist working against a background of established theories, knowledge, and technical training. But primitive or not, by Matisse's definition the painter of *Esther Tuttle* has done a creditable job of composition.

The rug, innocent of perspective, is drawn more like a decorated baseboard than fabric lying flat on the floor. This technical shortcoming is not important. The important thing is that the heavy curves of the rug's pattern are used in effective contrast with the crisp precision of the other forms. The pattern is, in fact, all the more vividly revealed for being free from the distortions that perspective would have introduced. If we insist on photographic realism we must admit that the artist has been totally unable to cope with the complications of the model's dress, but the important thing here is that the simple bell-like shape of the skirt is combined so happily with the nicely calculated, irregular puffs of the sleeves. The intricacy of the lace-trimmed collar is all the more effective for being played in fullest detail against the broad, undetailed silhouette of the dress. The wavering line of the bottom of the apron is one of the least conspicuous but most successful bits of design in the whole arrangement. Its gentle movement relieves the stiffness of the lower part of the figure without competing in interest with the upper part, where the face, drawn in profile with skillful delicacy, must hold its own against all this strong pattern. We have no way of knowing how accurate the drawing is as a likeness—it somehow looks very convincing—but the line is beautiful in itself.

Now you may feel that we are giving Joseph H. Davis credit for knowledge and talent he did not possess. But the fact remains that there are thousands of these primitive paintings, and for every one of such merit as the portrait of Esther Tuttle there are hundreds that are merely dull, inexpressive, and awkward.

There is certainly very little conscious application of theory or rule in this painting, and probably none at all. But every detail is carefully considered as part of the total arrangement, every detail is important to the total effect, and the total effect is good. It is too good to be merely a fortunate accident. The design is creative, even if it is arrived at through a feeling for rightness rather than by rule and theory. As we go on in these portfolios we will see that even when the most highly skilled painter applies rules and theories, it is still the feeling for rightness that makes the difference between a successful exercise and a work of art.

The attraction of a really good primitive painting is that the innate creative sensitivity of the artist speaks so directly and purely. It would certainly be a grotesque exaggeration to say that the portrait of Esther Tuttle is a great painting. The extreme smallness of the hands and feet may be as much the result of technical limitations as Davis's effort to show Miss Tuttle as a lady of refinement and delicacy. But anyone who looks at such a painting with as much perception as Davis employed in executing it will recognize that its merits lie deeper than its attractive quaintness. This primitive painter has, indeed, shown himself to be an artist in the arrangement, in a decorative manner, of the elements at his disposal.

Now we will compare the portrait of Esther Tuttle with three other two-dimensional portraits of women to show that the vocabulary of line, shape, and color is a flexible one. All three of these pictures are the work of masters of such established reputation that Davis would probably have quailed at the prospect of having to stand alongside them. Yet it is easy to believe that these men could have appreciated his artistry and, fully aware of its limitations, could have recognized its kinship to their own. One of these men is a seventeenth-century Japanese; another, a sixteenth-century court painter; and the third, one of the great revolutionaries of modern art. Their names are Kiyonobu, Holbein, and Matisse—who has already supplied our temporary working definition of composition.

Most of us can appreciate the quality of sincerity in a technically limited painting like *Esther Tuttle*. But it is harder for some of us to understand why an artist like Matisse chooses to work in a way that seems to deny his technical heritage. Matisse was a highly trained painter who discarded the whole tradition of "painting things the way they look." As a young unknown he augmented his income by copying old masters in the Louvre. These copies are irreproachable, and Matisse was capable of doing original work of the same technical caliber. But for him, original work in the manner of the old masters was no more satisfying than the making of copies. He set about finding a means of expression that

would be his own. Like most other great moderns he passed through the stage of technical dexterity to something beyond—but to many people his work looks inexplicably unskilled.

One reason people are puzzled by the art of Matisse is that they try to find the wrong things in it. You look for one thing in Rembrandt, another in Matisse. When he defined composition as arrangement "in a decorative manner," Matisse confessed a preoccupation with ornamental pattern that some critics consider a limitation. His work is sometimes more successful as decoration than as expression, just as we said Gozzoli's *Journey of the Magi* may be. Yet, Matisse himself has also said that the aim of composition is expression. "I am unable to distinguish between my feeling for life and the way I have of expressing it," he said, and his feeling for life, in that case, is one of gaiety, of elegance. These qualities, attractive if not profound, are represented at their highly civilized best in his *Lady in Blue* (Plate 51).

Lady in Blue

The freshness and the deceptive simplicity of *Lady in Blue* suggest that it must have been a spontaneous creation, easily achieved. But during its painting a day-to-day photographic record was kept of the stages through which it passed (*Figure 2*). These photographs show that *Lady in Blue* began as a semirealistic impression, went through many transformations, and became the picture we now see only after a series of drastic readjustments of its shapes and colors. Describing this method of work Matisse said: "Supposing I want to paint the body of a woman: first of all I endow it with grace and charm, but I know that something more than that is necessary. I try to condense the meaning of this body by drawing its essential lines. The charm will then become less apparent at first glance, but in the long run it will begin to emanate from the new image." So, if *Lady in Blue* does not appeal to you at

9

first, the only fair test is to get to know it over a period of time, to see whether in Matisse's "long run" the charm does begin to emanate from the final combination of shapes and colors that satisfied the artist.

The point we are making here, though, is that the unschooled painter of *Esther Tuttle* and the highly trained painter of *Lady in Blue*, working from the opposite poles of innocence and sophistication, share an essential similarity. The model, the dress, and the accessories in both paintings are only raw material for flat pattern that is ornamental and expressive in its own way in each picture. It may be easier for us to see the expressive power of *Esther Tuttle* because we can more easily sympathize with the struggles of the untrained painter and applaud his victory over technical handicaps. It is not so easy for most people to comprehend the technical and philosophical background that leads Matisse to reject all the skills Davis would have so liked to have had.

But there are some very direct similarities between the two pictures. In both of them the bell-like skirt is relieved by the uneven lines and masses of the blouse. The contrast between the intricate lace-trimmed collar and somber robe in *Esther Tuttle* is comparable to the same elements in the Matisse, substituting the jabot for the lace. Other similarities are apparent after a little examination. Whereas the primitive painter, unable to cope with the problem of perspective, has worked by necessity in two dimensions, Matisse has discarded

by intention the principles of perspective to capitalize on flat patterns.

The Esther Tuttle portrait is essentially a spotting of solid areas; the Matisse is this plus a balance of curves. The lyrelike yellow forms derived from the arms of a sofa are reversed in the curve of the light trim on the skirt. A series of arcs—the sides of the skirt, the edge of the red seat of the sofa, the black shapes in the background—is tied in with these S-shapes. The hand holding the beads is startling in size, and at first it is not as easy to accept this bigness as it is to accept the equally exaggerated littleness of the hands and feet of Esther Tuttle. But if you cover up this hand the picture looks empty. As a hand it would be grotesque, but it is not a hand. It is part of an arrangement of line and shape and color. Its extraordinary size and conspicuous position in the center of the picture make it the major stabilizing element in this composition of so many curves. The picture, in its final effect, is static. It is tranquil. "What I dream of is an art of balance, of purity and serenity devoid of troubling or depressing subject matter," Matisse said. If ever he achieved that dream he achieved it in *Lady in Blue*.

A Persian Miniature

Before proceeding to the next portrait of a woman we might pause to examine another painting related to our present theme. Matisse was strongly influenced by oriental art. Several

February 26, 1937   March 3, 1937   March 10, 1937   March 13, 1937   March 17, 1937

connections between *Lady in Blue* and the Persian miniature *Bahram Gur in the Turquoise Pavilion* (Plate 52) are immediately apparent. There is the same emphasis on silhouette rather than on the illusion, sought by Western artists, of solid, rounded forms; the same use of even, ungraduated color; and the same flattening out of perspective (or, more accurately, the same denial of perspective) so that the tile-paved floor, turned up as if it were the side of a wall, reveals its pattern without distortion. We have already pointed out these same resemblances between *Lady in Blue* and the portrait of Esther Tuttle. *Esther Tuttle* may bear an even closer resemblance to the Persian miniature style in these respects than *Lady in Blue*, for the Matisse cultivates an air of improvisation while the Persian miniature and the American primitive are both executed with all the precision the respective artists could manage. In Gozzoli's *Journey of the Magi* we saw that the landscape forms were decoratively, not realistically, conceived. This is true of *Bahram Gur in the Turquoise Pavilion* also, where trees and plants are designed, rather than imitated, from nature. In both pictures the forms "recede into the distance" in layers from the bottom to the top of the picture instead of lying behind one another in three-dimensional distance. But of the three Western pictures only the Matisse was painted with reference to the oriental conventions followed by the Persian miniaturists. The requirements of mural decoration dictated Gozzoli's

coincidental use of them; in the portrait of Esther Tuttle they were the natural result of limited knowledge in combination with a fine sensitivity to design. And *Esther Tuttle* bears another resemblance to the Persian miniature for the same reason: Davis has incorporated his identifying legend at the bottom of the picture in a decorative script that is quite intentionally in harmony with the picture itself. It is, essentially, a part of the picture. With more sophistication, as would be expected, but with the same feeling for decorative unity with the forms of the painting, the Persian artist has also incorporated in the miniature a script, one that seems more ornamental to our eyes because it is unfamiliar.

Two Japanese Prints

In our discussions of Picasso's *Demoiselles d'Avignon* in the preceding portfolio we said that the abstract and realistic elements in a painting may conflict to such an extent that our enjoyment of either one may be marred by the other. If you don't respond to *Lady in Blue* it is probably because no matter how hard you resist you keep looking for a realistic picture behind the highly abstract lines, shapes, and colors. There should be no such difficulty in a Japanese print by Kiyonobu I, *Woman Dancer with a Fan and Wand* (Plate 53). Never having developed our Western preoccupation with photographic reality, oriental painting at an early stage reached such a satis-

March 19, 1937   March 21, 1937   March 25, 1937   April 4, 1937   April 6, 1937

Figure 2

11

factory balance between subject and abstraction that our own extreme expression of realism and our corresponding extreme reaction into abstraction did not take place. Japanese and Chinese artists, working within a tradition of many centuries, perfected the expressive virtues of two-dimensional composition in which abstraction and subject matter are mutually supporting, not competing.

The sinuous yet strong lines and shapes of *Woman Dancer with a Fan and Wand* are a superb expression of the studied, flowing postures of the dance. Each line is interesting whether we take it for itself or as a part of the system of lines making up the whole figure. Long curving arcs come to a point and turn quickly into almost straight lines; a series of lines like those around the waist looks at first like a knotted convolution, but unwinds as we look at it into a system of perfectly clear, simple elements. But we look at no single line for very long. Each one catches us up into the stream of lines. The stream moves quickly here, slowly there, suggesting flowing water or drifting smoke. The pattern of flowers and leaves on the sleeve is a delight in itself, but it too is like a line in its over-all movement within a system of nearby lines. Some of the heavier forms are like weights or brakes to the quicker movement of the others. Our constant and increasing pleasure in these abstract patterns is always fused with the idea of the dancer's movements. We have the double pleasure of an identifiable subject and an abstract expression, coexisting in indissoluble harmony.

If you turn the illustration upside down, especially if you cover the face of the dancer, the design no longer represents a dancer's figure and becomes a purely abstract composition. It is completely changed, however, for it billows upward into a climax of heavy forms. Right side up, the heavier forms lie in the lower half of the picture and curve up through lighter ones to the delicacy of the head with its terminating hat and the fillip of the orange bow. This is planned, of course. But the same thing happens, either by plan or only by an awareness of its rightness, in *Esther Tuttle*, in which the delicate profile with its lightly painted bow at the neck and ornaments in the hair have a similar relationship to the heavier forms below.

As a brief aside before we see the Holbein, we can look at another Japanese woodcut, Kiyotada's *Actor Dancing* (Plate 54). We do not need the grimace of the face, nor the paraphernalia of the swords, which replace the fan and wand in the woman dancer's hands, to tell us that this is a dance of an entirely different character. We are told by line—sharp, angular line interrupted by other lines—and by individual shapes that are jagged and irregular instead of sinuous and flowing. The total silhouette has this same jagged character. The word harmony suggests, always, smoothness and grace. Actually, we have in *Actor Dancing* something like a harmony of conflicts—to be completely paradoxical—just as in music we may have a harmony of dissonances.

Two Princesses

After pictures of such extreme flatness as those we have been seeing, Holbein's *Christina of Denmark* (Plate 55) may not seem to fall within our two-dimensional bracket. We will show in a moment why we think it does. In the meantime, we need hardly observe that this portrait is by far the most realistic picture of our group. It may also be the subtlest as to composition, and it is the only one to use composition as a means of expressing an individual personality.

Upon one of the several occasions when Henry VIII was "between wives," this habitual royal widower was considering the princess Christina as successor to Jane Seymour, his third wife. Christina was reported to Henry to be a fascinating woman, but Henry, unwilling to take a chance on the lady's appearance, in 1538 sent Holbein to paint her portrait for his

12

Figure 3

inspection. The portrait charmed the king as it has charmed everybody ever since, but Christina was less charmed with Henry's reputation as a husband, and the union never materialized.

Fundamentally, Holbein's portrait is a composition of three light areas silhouetted against a dark field—first the oblong of paper pinned to the wall, then the oval face with its small frill of collar, and finally the hands with their white cuffs and glove. These three light silhouettes have a wonderful variety. The paper is simply a right-angled oblong. The hands, cuffs, and glove, in complete contrast, are combined into an irregular shape full of curves and projections—a beautiful piece of design in itself. The oval of the lovely face, terminated at the brow by the straight line of the cap and ornamented below by the lively frill of collar (*Figure 3*), makes a silhouette sharing the regularity of the paper's shape and the variety of the hands, cuffs, and glove.

It is no accident that the face and the oblong of paper share a common horizontal line through the center, while the face and hands share a corresponding vertical relationship. These two lines echo the top and sides of the panel, firmly anchoring the three floating shapes in the picture area. The face, naturally, comes at the intersection of these two lines, thus making certain that even if the features were less fascinating in themselves, it would still be the climax of the three shapes and hence the climax of the picture.

If the picture were made up only of these three shapes against a solid dark background, it would still be an effective composition. Variety, unity, and climax have seldom been so economically and harmoniously combined. But the arrangement also has a secondary theme: the silhouette of the robe against the background and the gentle rhythms of its fur-trimmed edge and the curving folds of the sleeves. These elements are kept rich and subdued in a most satisfying counterpoint to the sharp-edged clarity of the light shapes.

All this, however, does not quite explain the feeling we have that here is a real person, a person of great reserve, of acute intelligence—a subtle woman, a most attractive but not quite approachable one. What is it about the picture that suggests this personality? It is largely a question of arrangement; it is a matter of her pose and the placement of the figure in space.

Recalling the painting, even after having seen it frequently, you would probably have the impression that Christina is shown directly facing us in the center of the picture. Actually, however, the figure is turned slightly away on our left, and its axis (from the head along the opening of the gown to the floor) is well to the left of center. If the figure were truly centered it would relay to us the impression of a much more foursquare, more obvious, more everyday woman. As it is, the slight turn of the body and the slight variation from center constitute a removal from us—very slight it is true, but enough to make the direct gaze of the eyes all the more arresting. This off-centering of the picture could have produced an uncomfortable off-balance effect, but the unexpected white oblong of paper pulls enough interest toward the right to bring the arrangement back into stability. The result is balance, but balance with a greater feeling of life than we could have had if the figure, so static and reserved, had been placed absolutely frontally, in the absolute center.

To illustrate this point we can compare the portrait of the Danish princess with *Anne of Cleves* (Plate 56), which Holbein painted the following year (1539). The circumstances of its commission were the same: Henry, still shopping after Christina's refusal, sent Holbein to portray this runner-up among the candidates for the precarious honor of being queen of England.

It is an entrancing picture—possibly, in its elaboration of ornamental detail, more immediately attractive than the one of Christina. Presented with a different personality in his

14

Figure 4

sitter, Holbein responds with a contrasting composition. Anne is presented in an absolutely frontal position, centered on the canvas, in a design as nearly symmetrical as possible without monotony. The sweet, prim, guileless, and unimaginative little mask faces us patiently, with a suggestion of gentle obedience (*Figure 4*). The hands are clasped in a meek and compact little bundle (*Figure 5*), whereas Christina's were so beguilingly silhouetted (*Figure 6*). The elaborate robe, headdress, and jewels, so different from the rich but subdued elegance of Christina's costume, manage to invest the ordinary little person with an air of circumstance; in the long run the trappings are what we most notice and

remember, while we remember Christina as a woman. As an expression of character the portrait of Anne of Cleves is as successful a composition as the one Holbein devised to interpret Christina's fascinating and subtle personality; if it is less fascinating than Christina's, it is because it serves a less fascinating subject, showing us a sweet but unexceptional woman surrounded by and patiently accepting all the trappings of high position. These trappings flatter Anne. In a way the portrait was too successful: Henry liked it enough to contract the union but was so disappointed that he divorced Anne with indecent haste.

Now what are the rules for creating such compositions? There simply are none, except of the most general kind. Every artist knows that variety of shape makes for interest; that strong value contrast, that is, strong contrast between lights and darks produces heightened dramatic effect; that a psychological balance can be created between a large, rather heavy area like Christina's robed figure and a small but very light and conspicuous one like the paper on the wall back of her. But the final rightness of the disposition of the various elements in *Christina of Denmark* is the result of the same thing that made *Esther Tuttle* more than just another quaint primitive—the artist's sensitivity in applying the general principles.

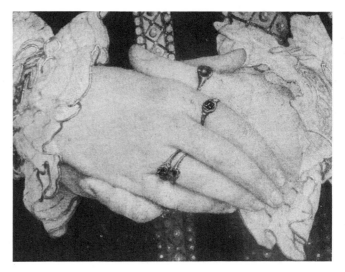

Composition in Theory and Practice

As we continue to analyze compositions we will find that certain rules, which will be discussed in the next portfolio, can be formulated for them, sometimes quite definitely. But we can never set down rules and formulas that will entirely explain the almost magical power some paintings have to satisfy and move us through their arrangements, even when they do follow rules. And it would be too bad if we could. From time to time some theorist— usually a third- or fourth-rate painter who wonders why his own pictures, painted by rule, are so poor—sets out to discover the compositional secrets of the old masters and reduce them to a foolproof mathematical basis. Some of the systems have stirred interest among painters and critics who should have known better. The trouble is that the systems work just as well when applied to commonplace pictures or objects as they do with great ones. Precise theories that pretend to explain the beautiful forms of Greek vases or architecture or great pictorial compositions also explain some of the unloveliest forms and dullest paintings ever created in exactly the same way, as if they were equally beautiful. Anyone who has taken a course in musical composition knows that it is possible to learn the rules of counterpoint and apply them correctly to produce a fugue that may be technically impeccable but downright ugly in sound. Composition in architecture, music, sculpture, or anything else is always a matter of creation, for which the rules are only a guide or skeleton.

When Holbein painted the Danish princess he applied no principles that he had not applied in other portraits, but *Christina of Denmark* is supreme in his work for its subtlety in the suggestion of personality. Occasionally his portraits are purely ornamental likenesses, always marvelously drawn and painted; we read the character of some others by deduction from features, facial expression, and even pose. But his greatest work combines these elements with compositional expressiveness: Christina lives for us so vividly not only because Holbein has reproduced her appearance with such wondrous skill but particularly because he has used composition to express her personality.

We have analyzed the portrait of Christina as a two-dimensional arrangement because, in spite of the realistic modeling, it is so conceived. Actually, the modeling is very slight. Although there is some indication of very shallow space, there is no effort to create a spatial illusion, which is a different thing alto-

Figure 6

gether. Logically explained, the piece of paper is pinned to the wall a foot or so back of the head, but compositionally the three light silhouettes perform on a single plane. However, we must always accept some ambivalence when a composition of modeled objects is conceived in what we might call "unmodeled space"; if you prefer to regard the picture in its very shallow third dimension, the general analysis of its composition as we have given it can still be applied without very much modification.

In either case, Matisse could have been writing of Holbein when he said: "The whole arrangement of my picture is expressive. The place occupied by figures or objects, the empty spaces around them, the proportions—everything plays a part. All that is not useful in a picture is detrimental." Everything in the painting of Christina is useful. Holbein's condensation of maximum expression into minimum means has preserved for us the personality of a sitter who was apparently just as fascinating as reports to Henry said she was. And in the case of the Anne of Cleves portrait, where the costume imposed upon the painter a great deal of detail, he in turn imposed upon that detail his own expressive formula: the reduction of all forms to a simple, well-defined silhouette, at once ornamental and interpretive.

In our next painting, *Saint Catherine* (Plate 57) by the Master of the Saint Lucy Legend, the compositional problem is reversed. Whereas Holbein restricts detail within certain areas, this medieval master revels in a prolixity of detail over the entire surface of his panel. His problem is not to find the perfect placement of a few perfect shapes, but to enrich his picture surface with as many shapes as possible and make them exist in harmony with one another.

Like Christina of Denmark, Saint Catherine is a noble lady richly attired. But unlike Christina she is hardly a unique personality in herself. She conveys to us nothing more than the gentle sweetness typical of whole bands of maiden saints. In a way, she serves the painter only as a manikin for the display of rich fabrics. But here is the difference: all this rich display is votive in character. Just as the medieval craftsman would encrust a holy object with rare jewels, so this painter seeks to cover every fraction of the panel's surface with an enrichment of shapes and colors of every kind, as if every new detail were an offering upon a shrine.

Christina of Denmark stirs our imagination; *Saint Catherine* leads us into an adventure of pure visual delight. Each object is as carefully rendered as if it were the most important one in the composition. Leaves, blossoms, golden hair, elaborate crown, book, curious little hands, brocade, ermine, sword, wall, ground, plants, lake, tiny swans, city wall, church tower, city buildings—each one is painted as if the success of the picture depended on it alone.

Such an accumulation of details must be held to some kind of organized discipline if the subject is not to be lost in a jumble of incidental attractions. This discipline is imposed by line. By "line" in this case we may mean an actual line made by the edge of a form, like the one made by the fold in the skirt running from the hem up to the hand holding the book. Or we may mean a suggested line, like the one implied by the sequence of the hands and head

17

Figure 7

of the pagan emperor who lies in defeat at the bottom of the picture. This suggested line is an important one compositionally, repeating as it does the line of the large curving fold of the skirt we have just mentioned (*Figure 7*).

The painter was more interested in creating this repeated line to unite the two figures than he was in putting the emperor's body into a reasonable attitude where it is hidden behind the saint's skirt. Out of sight in two-dimensional composition is frequently out of mind. The emperor's head appears from behind one side of our saint while his feet project from the other in a manner that leaves the position of the rest of his body ambiguous. If the painter had been thinking of his subjects in three dimensions, he would have conceived of the space back of the saint and the emperor's body as a solid form occupying it, and the relationship of head and feet would have been rational. But since the painter is organizing only the surface of his panel, it is enough for him that the hands and head of the emperor are adequately tied into the general surface scheme.

This scheme is based on the long pointed oval formed by the figure of the saint. We have already seen one major line emphasizing this oval—the heavy fold in the skirt. The line of this fold can be caught up again, after the slight interruption of the book, by following along the hair to the face and crown, back down the hair along the cape and sleeve on the other side, thus coming back down into the folds of the robe once more. Obviously, this line breaks, wavers, and occasionally wanders off into small, complicated excursions as in the pattern made by the skirt's ermine border, which is a nice piece of design in itself. But once we begin following this line or the others that run into and out of it, we discover that we are led from one delightful detail to another with just enough interruption to make the trip interesting. As if to brace these long easy rhythms, the painter has created a tripodlike scheme of three straight lines: two long straight folds in the skirt and the line of the sword, all meeting at the saint's right hand.

There is nothing very systematic about this tying together of the multitudinous details. The composition is a free invention along a general scheme dominated by the lines within the figure of the saint or other lines echoing them. But there are less conspicuous systems that also tie the picture together. If you notice the angle of the book you should be able to find it repeated in half a dozen places. The background, made up of a series of horizontal bands, forms a framework or trellis supporting the tapestrylike complications of ornamental details. Thus the painter is free to create a surface as elaborately rich and active as he wishes, while at the same time his total effect remains appropriately quiet and orderly.

We have said that every rich detail is like an offering to the demure little figure of the saint.

Figure 8

Yet it is still necessary that—as part of a picture—she hold her own against them. The painter has taken one more precaution to assure this. Sharply defined within the lines of her patterned bodice, her burnished hair, and her filigreed crown, the face and neck of the saint form an island of quietness on a picture surface that is busy everywhere else. This area is as close to being blank and unmodeled as it can be and still describe the saint's features. The brow, the cheek, and the neck are hardly more than flat color. We notice the face—as a picture area—simply because it is *not* elaborated. The little saint holds her own in this quiet way much as, in life, by virtue and piety she was invulnerable to the world's confusions.

Linear Rhythms

By now we have seen that line may be used for its own sake, or as the defining edge of a shape, or as a structural or expressive device. The same line may perform in several of these ways at once. In the art of the Italian renaissance painter Botticelli every function of line is integrated with every other one. Botticelli worked in Florence when the greatest excitement and the most modern art centered around developing the techniques of three-dimensional realism: perspective, light and shade, and accuracy of anatomical structure and proportion. Botticelli adopted all these discoveries as they appeared, but not wholeheartedly. His art resisted the new passion for realism, as if he had only grafted the new discoveries onto a dominating oriental tradition.

Of course Botticelli could not possibly have known the art of the Far East; he worked centuries earlier than the Japanese printmakers we have just seen. But he was as absorbed with the creation of linear rhythms as any oriental. The enjoyment of his almost eccentric style involves first of all an appreciation of line. Botticelli's line is his signature.

His *La Primavera*, or *Spring* (Plate 58), is an inexhaustible succession of linear inventions.

19

The subject is an allegory that has been given various interpretations. In the center the figure of Venus stands within a natural arch formed by a grove of trees (*Figure 8*). Above her hovers Cupid, and to the right one of the Hours enters scattering blossoms, ushered in by Flora and Zephyrus, the west wind. On the left the Three Graces are intertwined in a dancing rhythm that is picked up and terminated by the figure of Mercury.

The subject is charming and the allegorical interpretations are interesting, but subject or no subject, allegory or no allegory, each one of these figures or groups of figures could stand by itself, devoid of any meaning at all, as an abstract linear arabesque. A study of the head of one of the Three Graces (Plate 59) will bring us closer to a picture that is most rewarding at close range.

Botticelli's genius with line is immediately apparent in the design of the hair. Flowing locks and fluttering draperies are, of course, among the most obvious and most flexible subjects for linear treatment. But this coiffure is pure invention. Rationally examined, it is a physically impossible one. There is simply not room on the scalp for the masses of hair in this particular disposition, nor could any physical circumstance produce or maintain these flowing convolutions. But of course we are not looking at hair or at a coiffure. We are looking at lines, and lines that have their own grace and logic as they flow into and out of one another.

Their beauty is apparent enough not to need analysis. But we are not so likely to notice the less spectacular lines of the rest of the figure: the profile, neck, and shoulders in our detail. They are even more subtly controlled than those of the hair. Following them we find contours just as graceful and just as inventive, but stronger, quieter, more reserved. The strength and gravity of their curves serve as foils to the more fluid, rapidly moving lines nearby. Where the jaw divides from the neck Botticelli has placed a quite arbitrarily straight line. It

is repeated by two almost straight ones across the neck just below it and is finally picked up by the line of the shoulder, where it is carried on into the strong, quiet one of the upper arm.

The area within these contours is modeled, yet it is their determining outline rather than the modeled form that tells. For that matter, the bounding lines are adequately expressive of the form between them without the assistance of modeling.

Are the lines in *La Primavera* expressive ones? Yes: the picture is a lyrical celebration of grace, refinement, and sensitivity to the beautiful. We can use these same words to describe the linear character: its beauty lies in its grace, its refinement, its sensitivity. And, we should add, its strength. It is particularly in this strength that Botticelli's line lives, whereas that of his imitators turns sagging and flaccid. The line of *La Primavera* is expressive because it is appropriate. It is perfectly integrated with the idea the picture is trying to convey.

Linear Rhythms as Structures

The lines are also structural. A series of swag-like ones runs through the composition from one figure to another. One of these can be followed from the shoulder of Zephyrus down his arm, along the bent arm of the central figure of the group, up along the arm, neck, and head of the Hour, then along the tree trunk back of her into the archlike form encircling Venus—thus leading us to the picture's climactic figure. Or we can follow another, larger swag beginning at the same place, but following this time Flora's lowered arm, then along a fluttering hem, and up into the curve of Venus's red robe, and thus again to her head.

On the opposite side, a swag begins with the upraised arm of Mercury, follows down along his robe and the sword, and then up into the inexhaustible rhythms of the figures of the Three Graces. It is also possible to sense in a general way a swag stretching from one side of the picture to the other between the figures

Photo by Alinari

Figure 9

Figure 10

of Mercury and Zephyrus, although this general line is full of interruptions and reversals. This long, downcurving line is countered by the sturdier upward arched form of the trees in the center.

The picture also builds up into a tentlike peak at the middle, reaching an appropriate climax at the head of Venus. Again, the line is more obvious on the right than on the left side of the composition. The angle of the central figure of the group at the right is continued by foliage and tree trunks up to the figure of Cupid. Cupid's arm and arrow direct us firmly along a corresponding angle. We are again interrupted by the inescapable complications of the Three Graces (*Figure 9*), but the line follows in a general way from Cupid's arrow to the feet of Mercury. It is echoed by Mercury's forearm nearest the Graces and by the line of his side above the hand on his hip. Some of these connections are tenuous, but they are there, and they should suggest other connections that you may be interested in discovering for yourself. All these various systems are superimposed, and frequently a single detail will perform its function simultaneously in more than one of them.

William Blake's *The Wise and Foolish Virgins* (*Figure 10*) incorporates several of the compositional devices we have been discussing and adds another. More than in any other picture we have seen so far, it uses line as a narrative factor. *The Wise and Foolish Virgins* is a storytelling picture; superficially the story is told by the images that act it out, but fundamentally by the lines composing them.

On the left of the picture stand the five wise virgins, their lamps glowing with the oil they have been wise enough to save against the coming of judgment. Ranged in righteousness, they reject the hysterical pleas of the unwise sisters who have squandered their oil and are now terrified by the sounding of the last trump in the sky.

The two groups are contrasted first by line. If you follow the lines of the wise virgins from toe to head, from the left edge of the picture to the figure with upraised arm, you will see that there is a gently increasing movement from one to the next. The first figure stands quite straight. The final one stands in an arc-shaped attitude. The figures between them are described by lines that make a gentle transition between the two. The movement from figure to figure is steady, confident, and serene.

By contrast, the lines of the group of the unwise five are wildly agitated, constantly interrupted, meeting at sharp angles instead of continuing to flow in graceful assurance. The kneeling figure in front has a strong movement toward the left. The others move in contradiction to the right. The whole arrangement of the group expresses confusion and distraction.

Much of this story we could read purely in the attitudes assumed by the figures, although of course Blake invents these attitudes for the purpose of exploiting them in line. But the keynote of the narrative is that the unwise virgins appeal to the wise to share their oil and are firmly refused—they must continue to suffer within their own foolishness. This idea is projected to us by line in this way: the kneeling figure appeals to the upright virtuous one, but this strong forward-rushing movement of appeal is turned back by the line of her own upraised hand, which swings us into the irrevocable line of the wise virgin's outstretched arm and back into the confusions of the group of unfortunates. This point of turning back is the climax of the composition. There is no return now into the fold of virtue. The unwise virgins are unequivocally rejected.

The two groups are contrasted by their line systems, one serene, one agitated, and are separated at the point of contact, where the upward rush of lines of the appealing figure breaks against the standing figure and must return. In its arc-shape, the upright figure seems to bend slightly against the agitated rush, but does not yield. However, the picture must not be allowed to break entirely in half, even though its two sides express opposing ideas. We cannot miss how the line of the supplicating hand is turned back along the extended arm. But, in a brilliant touch, this hand is also used to connect the two groups in a way Blake has been careful to make inconspicuous. The line of this hand is continued in the line of the wise virgin's scarf, though we must jump the barrier of the extended arm to follow it. The main line runs along the extended arm and back into the hysterical regrets of the foolish virgins, but through the secondary one we may re-enter the line system of the wise maidens. Thus the two groups are united, as they have to be in a well-knit composition, but they are also divorced, as they must be to tell this particular story of wisdom and folly.

23

The Art of the Poster

Before we conclude this portfolio we must mention one form of art that surrounds us every day, the art of the poster, by which we mean also the billboard, the full-page magazine advertisement, or any advertisement involving the putting together of lines and colors and shapes. For every picture we look at as a work of art we see a thousand posters, most of them blatant disfigurements of the city, the country-side, or the paper they are printed on. No art form is more abused. But at its best it can offer real aesthetic pleasure—and be all the more effective as a commercial medium for this reason.

The first illustration in this portfolio was a mural, where a two-dimensional scheme was imposed on the painter by the nature of the job he was commissioned to do. A similar restriction is imposed on the poster artist. Taking exceptions for granted, the general rule is that a good poster design is two-dimensional, for the pictorial image must be combined with type, which is necessarily quite flat. As a three-dimensional image combined with type or lettering of any kind is likely to be flattened out to make the type or lettering emphatically conspicuous, an image conceived in the first place to be most effective in two dimensions is likely to form a more harmonious union with the typography.

No poster is going to be as complicated as any of the pictures we have been discussing, simply because the job of the poster is to carry its message at a glance. It is not supposed to be constantly more rewarding on further acquaintance, since it is here today and gone tomorrow. Even so, a few posters have reached such stature as works of art that they have ended up in museums. The best known of these—probably the best-known posters in the world—are those of a French painter of the end of the nineteenth century, Henri de Toulouse-Lautrec. Toulouse-Lautrec's posters deserve their place in museums not only be-cause they are works of art but also because they are historically important. They are landmarks in our discovery that it is possible for a poster to be a work of art.

Japanese prints similar to those we saw at the beginning of this portfolio were a direct influence on posters like *Aristide Bruant in His Cabaret* (Plate 60). Bruant was a singer of popular ballads in cabarets that corresponded, more or less, to our night clubs. In a costume of black boots, black wide-brimmed hat, voluminous cloak, and scarf and cane, he sang the songs of the people of the streets in the argot, or popular slang, of Montmartre. Toulouse-Lautrec captures the professional personality of the singer, making no effort to reveal anything about the man himself, as a pure portrait would have done.

Since there is no time for the passer-by to appreciate subtleties of design like those in the Japanese prints, Toulouse-Lautrec goes far-ther and reduces the pattern to a minimum of shapes, capitalizing on strong flat areas of color and a few emphatic lines. It was said of his posters that they "took possession of the streets," which is certainly an indication of their commercial effectiveness. But wherever commercial expenses are involved in anything as variable and as personal as a work of art, there will always be opposition to risking money on anything new. As Toulouse-Lautrec's big, simple posters were something new, he usually designed them free or even bore some of the cost of printing to assure that they would finally appear exactly as he had designed them. Commercial art has to struggle against two degrading forces: a simple lack of taste or knowledge, which may be understandable and excusable, and the idea that public taste is so debased that for a mass market bad design may actually be more effective than good design simply because it is what people are accustomed to. The appalling truth is that for the first time in history bad art may be sought out for its badness, or created in the first place as bad art to supply a demand for

The Metropolitan Museum of Art

Figure 11

it. But fortunately this extreme is accompanied by the happier truth that commercial art at its best reaches a level today where it merges with fine art, as Toulouse-Lautrec's posters showed it could do (*Figure 11*).

In *Aristide Bruant* we see line, shape, and color used more purely as pattern than in any of the other illustrations in this portfolio, but our first illustrations were also pattern, ac-

companied by varying degrees of expressiveness. In the later illustrations, *Saint Catherine*, *La Primavera*, and *The Wise and Foolish Virgins*, we also saw line used as a structural element that tied together some fairly complex patterns. Our next portfolio will deal with pictures as structures, and we will go from flat structures into three-dimensional ones, with their attendant complications and satisfactions.

Notes on the Painters

Benozzo Gozzoli, 1420-1497, Italian

49. Detail from THE JOURNEY OF THE MAGI, ABOUT 1459

Fresco. Height of detail about 9'. Medici-Riccardi Chapel, Florence

Photo by Anderson

Benozzo was an industrious Florentine painter with a great decorative flair. While his artistic contemporaries were enthusiastically making technical discoveries that revolutionized Western painting, Benozzo was content to follow in their wake, using the discoveries that were convenient for his own purposes.

Such an unflattering introduction, which judges Benozzo in comparison with some of the greatest painters who ever lived, is not quite fair to him. The combination of decorative pattern and lively anecdote in his work has great attraction; it is pleasant to look at and unnecessary to think about. His subject is always happily presented; no matter how grandiose nominally, it is always enacted by charming figurines rather than by human beings, gods, or heroes. *The Journey of the Magi* is his most impressive work, although here too the dominant impression is one of festivity. Charm, gaiety, and decorative invention are second-rate virtues if you wish, but they are still virtues, and within them Benozzo is at the top in his field.

The rich trappings in *The Journey of the Magi* were inspired by those of Eastern potentates and their retinues who actually visited Italy in 1439. The journey of the Magi was traditionally a subject calling for the invention of rich costumes in luxurious fabrics—the silks and velvets of the East. The ceremonies and pageants connected with the visit of the Eastern dignitaries supplied Benozzo with live models, and he made the most of it, even to the extent of including portraits of two of the visitors, the Emperor of Byzantium and the Patriarch of Constantinople, as two of the Magi. For the third, the one in our illustration, he chose the young son of the house of Medici, Lorenzo, later called The Magnificent. Benozzo's own portrait is included in Lorenzo's retinue, along with those of other members of the Medici family.

Joseph H. Davis, active 1832-1837, American

50. ESTHER TUTTLE, 1836

Water color on paper. Height 11¾". The New-York Historical Society

Davis is one of hundreds of American primitive painters whose names are known. Many of these are known by only one or two signed pictures, not necessarily of much acknowledged or potential importance. A few of these unschooled artists, like Edward Hicks, who painted *The Peaceable Kingdom* (Plate 9, Portfolio 1), are prominently established as artists of importance represented by a large number of works. Davis is one of them. The portrait *Esther Tuttle* was recently attributed to him on the basis of "internal evidence," a phrase that can include style, calligraphy, the repetition of motives, or perhaps geographical identification of the picture or subject establishing a strong likelihood of its authorship. More than a hundred water colors, all portraits executed between 1832 and 1837, are now identified with this painter.

Henri Matisse, 1869-1954, French

51. LADY IN BLUE, 1937

Oil on canvas. Height 36½". Mrs. John Wintersteen, Philadelphia

If the list of dominant figures in European painting for the first half of the twentieth century had to be reduced to two, Matisse would have to be named with Pablo Picasso. Between them they represent the two aspects of the departure from representational form that is the basis of the modern revolt. Picasso, in cubism, began with the idea of analyzing form by breaking it up and recombining it in new ways. Matisse, in fauvism, began with the idea of distorting form in any way he pleased in order to express his own emotional experience.

Fauvism derives from the French word *fauve*, meaning wild beast. It was originally used as a term of derision for a group of painters who worked in brilliant, pure colors and departed freely from visual truth to increase the range of personal expression. The fauve group, formed in 1905, included Georges Rouault, whose *Two Nudes* (Plate 28) was discussed in Portfolio 3. Fauvism was a movement receptive to individual variation. At one extreme is *Two Nudes*, with its expressive intensity; at the other, *Lady in Blue*, with its concentration on happier mood and more sophisticated and fashionable overtones.

In the end, this is the mood that most generally permeates the art of Matisse. It is particularly felicitous in *Lady in Blue*. A picture like this one shows why Matisse is so frequently regarded as the direct heir of a long French tradition that reached an apogee in the eighteenth century, the tradition that is denigrated by the description "boudoir painting." It is a tradition in which a large part is played by feminine sensitivities, a tradition of elegance and vivacity, degenerating now and then into mere chic, a tradition that is never concerned with moral or social values. It is easy to dismiss such a tradition in favor of one with more pretentious goals, even when these goals are less expertly achieved. It is easy, too, to take for granted its end effect of lightness and charm without recognizing the discipline and craftsmanship that may go into its production.

In the case of Matisse it is particularly easy for the layman to make this mistake since his art looks so easy to do. In the body of the text we have reproduced photographs of *Lady in Blue* in some of its preliminary stages and have tried to explain some of Matisse's compositional theories. In a more extended consideration of his art it would be possible to illustrate earlier paintings in which his disciplined study of form is more apparent, largely because he had not yet achieved the almost reflexive mastery over it that marks work like the *Lady in Blue*. In the end, however, *Lady in Blue* should appeal, as Matisse intended it to do, in a very immediate way to our responses to color and form as elements of delight, without too much analyzing or intellectualizing as to why they delight us.

We might mention here that Renoir, represented in Portfolio 1 by *Madame Renoir* and *In the Meadow* (Plates 3 and 4), is also thought of as a painter stemming at least in part from the so-called "boudoir tradition," a term that does only limited justice to a style of painting that, beyond its elegant, feminine delicacy, is also characterized by real sensitivity and strength. Renoir's preoccupation is with simple values rather than sophisticated ones, with the burgeoning countryside instead of the hothouse, with woman as a symbol of fertility rather than woman as an erotic ornament—but it is still true that he paints in the same tradition. He is concerned with sensuous delight rather than with psychological, philosophical, or sociological analysis, and his technical inheritance from the boudoir masters of the eighteenth century is great. Of a painting by Francois Boucher, the most typical master of the school, Renoir says, "I keep coming back to it as one returns to a first love." Matisse could almost have said the same thing. As time goes on and Matisse's departure from the kind of representation to which we are accustomed seems less extreme, his connection with the art of the eighteenth century will probably be as apparent as Renoir's is now.

Shaikh-zada of Khurasan (?), XVI century, Persian

52. BAHRAM GUR IN THE TURQUOISE PAVILION (miniature painting from a manuscript of Nizami's Khamsa, dated 1524-25)

Tempera on paper. Height 7¼". The Metropolitan Museum of Art, gift of Alexander Smith Cochran, 1913

The greatest of all Persian painters was one Bihzad, whose work began to appear about 1480. The miniature reproduced in this portfolio is from one of the finest Persian manuscripts in this country, a copy of the Khamsa of Nizami, dated 1525, which is in Bihzad's style. There are fine points of difference from his style—the composition is a little freer and the figures a little more supple than Bihzad would have made them—but his general manner and his palette have been retained by Shaikh-zada, the artist to whom this painting is attributed. Persian painting was a highly traditional and formalized art. Bihzad seems to have been the first to go directly to nature for much of his inspiration. Although to Western eyes *Bahram Gur in the Turquoise Pavilion* is formalized in the extreme, it is graceful and intimate in comparison with the stock compositions that were handed down from teacher to pupil, generation after generation, with very little allowance for originality, before Bihzad made his contribution.

This particular manuscript, formerly in the Persian royal library, left that country in the early years of this century when the ruler was suffering financial embarrassment. It is said that when his ladies became particularly importunate he would give them a volume from the royal library, telling them to sell it for whatever they could get and buy themselves new dresses or jewelry with the proceeds. No doubt many fine Persian manuscripts and other works of art thus found their way to the West.

Torii Kiyonobu I, 1664-1729, Japanese

53. WOMAN DANCER WITH A FAN AND WAND, ABOUT 1708

Hand-colored woodcut. Height 21¾". The Metropolitan Museum of Art, Dick Fund, 1949

Torii Kiyotada, active 1710-1740, Japanese

54. ACTOR DANCING, ABOUT 1715

Hand-colored woodcut. Height 11¼". The Metropolitan Museum of Art, Dick Fund, 1949

Kiyonobu I and Kiyotada are leaders of the early *Ukiyoye* school of Japanese printmaking. *Ukiyoye* may be translated as "Pictures of the Floating World," and, for all the refinement and even esoteric quality that mark this school for the average Western eye, for the Japanese it was a popularization of art, the first popular expression in the then thousand-year-old tradition of Japanese art. The development occurred for the usual sound reason: plebeians were prosperous enough to support it. Visitors to Tokyo (then Edo), the new military capital of the shogunate government, took *Ukiyoye* prints home as souvenirs. Famous sights, festivals, leading courtesans, and above all the actors of the popular theater were the subjects. Albums of erotic subjects also sold well.

Kiyonobu I was the son of a painter of theatrical signboards. The exceptional vigor of Kiyonobu's style continues to suggest the boldness of such work. Kiyotada, working a generation later, is represented today by only a few surviving prints. One writer has pointed out that his *Actor Dancing* suggests contemporary abstract painting in its geometrical design. It is reproduced in this portfolio at a fraction under exact size, but Kiyonobu's

Woman Dancer, an exceptionally large print, is reduced to about half its dimensions. Both were printed in black and colored by hand. (Japanese print processes are mentioned further in Portfolio 10.)

Hans Holbein the Younger, 1497-1543, German

55. CHRISTINA OF DENMARK, 1538

   Oil and tempera on wood. Height 70". The National Gallery, London

56. ANNE OF CLEVES, 1539-40

   Oil and tempera on parchment mounted on canvas. Height 26". The Louvre Museum, Paris

Holbein painted religious subjects as well as portraits, but it is as a portraitist that he is exceptional. Portrait painting is seldom the most rewarding field for an artist in the scope allowed for expression. There are obvious limitations imposed by the sitter himself and by the necessity to please the sitter. The work of most great painters is studded with an occasional great portrait; the work of Holbein includes occasional subject pictures among the unparalleled company of his portraits.

A German painter, he spent two periods of his career in England, first between 1520 and 1528 and then for the eleven years before his death in 1543. Both times he was in the service of Henry VIII. A good part of the completeness with which we are able to visualize this particular reign in England's history must be credited to Holbein. His dozens of paintings and drawings of members of the court convey personalities so vividly that history comes alive at the sight of them.

In the German-Swiss city of Basel, which was his home from early boyhood, Holbein was a friend of the philosopher Erasmus, of whom he did a number of portraits. Holbein also designed stained glass, woodcuts, and decorations—in fact his first call to England was on a commission to do the decorations for one of the king's festivals. None of his decorations remain, but the existing studies for those in the town hall at Basel are lively inventions.

His father, Hans Holbein the Elder, is also a painter of importance, but stylistically the two men are separated by more than a generation. The father remains closely allied with the early German school; the son is a painter of the Renaissance.

Photo by Archives Photographiques, Paris

Master of the Saint Lucy Legend, active 1470-1490, Flemish

57. SAINT CATHERINE

   Oil on wood. Height 26¼". The John G. Johnson Collection, Philadelphia

Like other anonymous painters, the Master of the Saint Lucy Legend, formerly known as the Master of Bruges of 1480, is identified by reference to his most important work, a three-paneled altarpiece in Bruges representing the legend of Saint Lucy. Other works, like *Saint Catherine*, are attributed to him by the kind of internal evidence mentioned in the discussion of the American primitive, Joseph H. Davis. This particular anonymous master is characterized by grace and sweetness in combination with elaborate ornamental detail.

Sandro Botticelli, 1444/45-1510, Italian

58. LA PRIMAVERA (SPRING), ABOUT 1478

Tempera on wood. Height 6'7¾". The Uffizi Gallery, Florence

59. Head of one of the Three Graces from LA PRIMAVERA

Photo by Alinari

Photo by Alinari

Botticelli painted *La Primavera* about 1478 for a Medici villa at Castello. With its equally celebrated companion piece in the Uffizi, *The Birth of Venus*, it is a masterpiece in his happiest style. Botticelli is one of the most individual of all painters, not only in his style, whose linear arabesques occupied us in this portfolio, but in his highly personal mood. Even more than other renaissance artists he was equally a master of the expression of pagan classical subjects and mystical Christian ones. In both areas his interpretation is distinctively his own. Classicism in the work of other early Florentine painters was largely intellectual, but in Botticelli's it is also sensuous and hence more complete. The particular stamp of his pictorial personality is a nostalgic languor, a sadness or even a foreboding, that runs beneath the most joyous subjects, like *La Primavera*. This mood would be cloying without Botticelli's reserve, which sometimes reaches the point of austerity, just as his flowing line would turn limp and monotonous without the indefinable nervous strength that is its basic characteristic. During the mid-nineteenth century Botticelli was rediscovered after a period of critical neglect and was much imitated in swooningly romantic pictures by certain members of a group of English painters called the Pre-Raphaelites. If they accomplish nothing else, these pseudo-Botticellis should, by comparison, reveal to any doubter the masculine force that makes Botticelli a great painter instead of a sentimentalist.

Botticelli's Christian subjects are particularly marked by this mood of foreboding. While other Florentines, including his master Fra Filippo Lippi, were representing the Madonna as a sweet mortal Italian girl, reverent and joyous with her healthy first-born, Botticelli's Madonnas regard the Child in full knowledge of the inevitable tragedy and glory of the Crucifixion.

Botticelli's presentiments of the transience of human joy were corroborated in the disorders that beset Florence at the end of the century. His great patron Lorenzo de' Medici, the Magnificent, died; in what amounted to a period of civil war the family, which had dominated Florence in its greatness, was exiled from the city; in the ensuing disruptions the city fell under the influence of the fanatic evangelist-monk Savonarola; finally, in an act of the most ignoble cruelty Savonarola was convicted of heresy, hanged, and burned. Botticelli had been a follower of Savonarola, and during this last period his Christian subjects are strained with mystical emotionalism to the verge of hysteria (but not beyond), and his few classical references are no longer lyrically pagan but are allegories of good and evil. (The great allegory of this period, *Calumny*, will be discussed in Portfolio 11 of this series.)

Henri de Toulouse-Lautrec, 1864-1901, French

60. ARISTIDE BRUANT IN HIS CABARET, 1893

Lithograph. Height 51⅛". The Metropolitan Museum of Art, Dick Fund, 1923

Toulouse-Lautrec, as the descendant of the Counts of Toulouse, inherited a name a thousand years old. He might never have been more than a Sunday painter and might have spent his life continuing the tradition of sport and horsemanship at the family seat in Albi, if it had not been for the childhood accidents in which his legs were broken. A deficiency in bone structure left Lautrec not a dwarf, but a dwarflike creature with the legs of a child and the powerful torso of a man, topped by a large head with gross features that belied his real sensitivity.

His life is known to most people today through faulty biographies, sensationalized pseudopsychiatric tracts, an unpardonably distorted movie, and a few books and articles in which his tragic and fantastic story is studied with respect. Toulouse-Lautrec was an alcoholic and led a life of flagrant dissipation. This is not surprising. What is surprising is that before he died at thirty-seven he had also produced a body of drawings, paintings, and prints that would have done credit to a vigorous, physically normal, psychologically unhounded man during a lifetime of full span.

Toulouse-Lautrec led not so much a "double life," with its implication of secret alternation between worthy and unworthy levels, as several lives at once and inseparably. As the inheritor of one of the oldest titles in France he was an eligible participant in the life of the *haut monde*, one that did not interest him very much. As a painter of talent and originality he was accepted and admired by other painters and by those critics and members of the public who, by the end of the century, had recovered from nineteenth-century academic paralysis. As an intellectual and wit he was at home in literary company, and as an inhabitant of Parisian bohemia he was a friend of everybody from the most prominent actors and entertainers to the madames and prostitutes in whose establishments he was a familiar. There was yet another world he inhabited alone, the private world of Henri de Toulouse-Lautrec the cripple, whose spiritual and physical pain he shared with no one else. It was from this world that he painted his wonderfully observant pictures of the others.

In Paris during the 1890s Toulouse-Lautrec preserved in pictures the most transient of all arts, that of the theater and dance hall with its actors, dancers, singers, clowns, and audiences. The *Aristide Bruant* poster comes from this world. In a later portfolio on the artist as a social critic and in another concerned with various technical processes (in the case of Toulouse-Lautrec, the lithograph) the art of this extraordinary man is further discussed.